SEC[OF Rain Forest

by Edward Myers

Modern Curriculum Press

Parsippany, New Jersey

Credits

Illustrations: 8–9: Mapping Specialists, Ltd. 13, 14: Jennifer DiRubbio. 18–19: Paul Bachem. 23: Jennifer DiRubbio. 42: Mapping Specialists, Ltd.

Photos: Front & back cover, Title page: Brian Kenney. 5: Nigel Press/Tony Stone Images. 6: l. Mark J. Thomas/Dembinsky Photo Associates; r. Brian Kenney. 7: t.l., r. Brian Kenney; m.l. E.R. Degginger/Color-Pic, Inc. 11, 12: Brian Kenney. 15: Bruce Forster/Tony Stone Images. 16: Brian Kenney. 17: ©Leonide Principe/Photo Researchers, Inc. 20: Anthony Fiala/National Geographic Society. 21, 22: Frans Lanting/Tony Stone Images. 24: ©Victor Englebert/Photo Researchers, Inc. 25: l. Will & Deni McIntyre/Tony Stone Images; r. ©Fletcher & Baylis/Photo Researchers, Inc. 26: Robert & Linda Mitchell. 27: ©Nigel Cattlin/Holt Studios International/Photo Researchers, Inc. 29: Brian Kenney. 30: Russ Gutshall/Dembinsky Photo Associates. 31: Robert W. Madden/National Geographic Society. 32: Paul A. Zahl, Ph.D./National Geographic Society. 33: Art Wolfe/Tony Stone Images. 34: t. Brian Kenney; b. Schafer & Hill/Tony Stone Images. 35: David McNew/Peter Arnold, Inc. 36: Robert & Linda Mitchell. 37: Art Wolfe/Tony Stone Images. 38: Sue Cunningham/Tony Stone Images. 39: Victor Englebert. 40: Kevin Schafer/Tony Stone Images. 41: ©Jacques Jangoux/Photo Researchers, Inc. 43: David Hiser/Tony Stone Images. 45: Fotopic/Omni-Photo. 46: ©Will & Deni McIntyre/Photo Researchers, Inc.

Cover and book design by Agatha Jaspon

ISBN 0-7652-0898-9

DRA® and Developmental Reading Assessment® are registered trademarks of Pearson Education, Inc.

Printed in the United States of America
10 11 12 13   07 06 05

Modern
Curriculum
Press

Pearson Learning Group

1-800-321-3106
www.pearsonlearning.com

CONTENTS

CHAPTER 1

What Is a Rain Forest?

Imagine a strange, beautiful planet. One of this planet's most amazing places is a "hot zone" around its middle. Some places in this hot zone have a warm, wet climate all year long. It's a good place for living things. All kinds of plants and animals call this place home. They have lived here for millions of years.

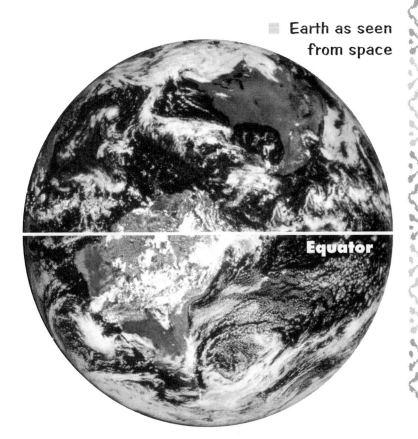

Earth as seen from space

Equator

In this place there's a deer the size of a rabbit, a frog that flies, and a spider that eats birds. There's a freshwater fish 8 feet long and a cow that lives in the water.

There's a bird with a beak almost as long as its body and a rodent that looks like a 100-pound guinea pig. There are trees that are hundreds of feet tall and plants that eat bugs.

Red-eyed tree frog

Animals of the rain forest

Tarantula

Tapir

Black hercules beetle

Neotropical plant bug

This planet is our own Earth. A special ecosystem called the rain forest is found in the hot zone. An ecosystem is all the plants and animals that live in a certain place. A rain forest is an area that has many different kinds of plants and other living things. It also has a high average temperature and lots of rain.

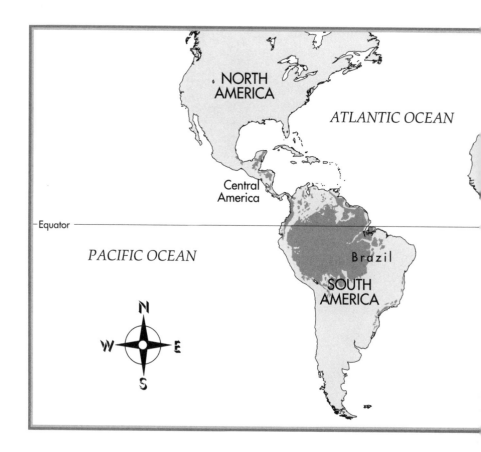

Most rain forests are tropical. This means they are located in a narrow band along the equator. The equator is an imaginary line that runs around the middle of the earth. The Amazon rain forest in South America is the largest in the world.

Map of rain-forest areas

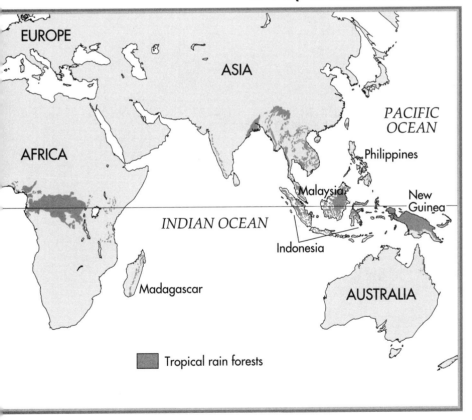

EUROPE

ASIA

PACIFIC OCEAN

AFRICA

Philippines

Malaysia

New Guinea

INDIAN OCEAN

Indonesia

Madagascar

AUSTRALIA

Tropical rain forests

Rain forests cover only a small part of the earth's surface. Yet they are home to more kinds of plants and animals than anywhere else. Many of these plants and animals are still unknown. They are like secrets waiting to be discovered deep in the forest.

Forest Facts

- Rain forests have been on Earth since the time of the dinosaurs.

- Because they have existed for so long, rain forests contain about half of all living things found on Earth.

◇ CHAPTER 2 ◇

Why Are Rain Forests So Important?

Tropical rain forests are home to more kinds of animals and plants than any other place on Earth. This is because the climate here has stayed nearly the same for almost 100 million years.

■ Imperial moth and plumed basilisk

The temperature is always about the same, so the forest is never too hot or too cold. There is always plenty of water to drink because rain falls almost every day.

In other parts of the world, the climate has changed many times over millions of years. Each time there was a major change, many kinds of plants and animals died.

Even if a species, or kind of animal or plant, lives through a climate change, it may not survive. Plants and animals need each other to live. There is a "web of life" that connects all species throughout the planet and in each ecosystem.

Baby spider monkey eating pokeweed berries

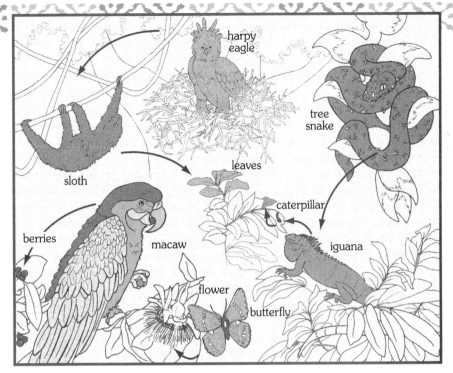

Rain-forest food web

For example, some insects eat plants or parts of plants. Birds then eat the insects. Other animals eat the birds. If one species in this web of life should die out, other species may die out, too, because they don't have food.

The trees and plants in the rain forests are more than food for animals. They are also homes for many kinds of living things. If the trees die, the animals that depend on them for shelter may also die.

13

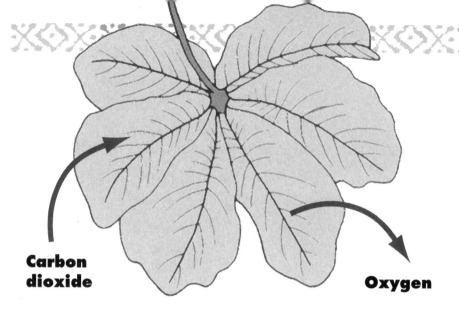

Carbon dioxide

Oxygen

A leaf takes in carbon dioxide and releases oxygen.

In addition, the rain forests are important because the leaves of the trees and plants act a little like the earth's lungs. How does this happen?

People and land animals use their lungs to breathe in air. They need a part of the air called oxygen to survive. People and animals then breathe out a part of the air they don't need. This part is called carbon dioxide.

Plants are just the opposite. They take in and use carbon dioxide to survive. They don't need much oxygen, which they release into the air. So plants increase the amount of oxygen in the air for people and animals to breathe. They also lower the amount of carbon dioxide.

Cars, planes, power plants, and factories also release carbon dioxide and other substances into the air. These substances pollute the atmosphere. If too much pollution is released, the atmosphere becomes warmer. If the earth's atmosphere becomes too hot, living things will not be able to survive.

The many plants and trees in the rain forests help to remove carbon dioxide from the air. They help keep the earth's climate at a comfortable temperature.

Pollution from a factory

15

Another reason the rain forests are so important is because they are home to many of the most amazing creatures and plants in the world. Today, scientists believe that they have been able to study only a small number of all rain-forest species. New species are being discovered all the time.

Forest Facts

There are very few golden lion tamarins left in the rain forest. Some tamarins are being raised by people and then taught to live in the forest.

CHAPTER 3

Who Discovered the Rain Forests?

The rain forests have been on Earth for millions of years. That is much longer than human beings have been here. How did people discover the rain forests?

The first people came into the rain forests thousands of years ago. They were in small groups, looking for food and places to live.

In South America, Amerindians traveled down into the rain forests from farther

A rain-forest child fixes a bow.

north. Many of them settled along the Amazon River.

Map of the route that Orellana took along the Amazon in search of food

About 500 years ago a Spanish explorer named Vicente Yáñez Pinzón (peen ZOHN) sailed to the coast of what is now Brazil. He saw where the Amazon River flows into the ocean, but he did not go into the rain forest.

In 1541, Gonzalo Pizarro (pih ZAHR oh), a Spanish soldier, traveled to the Andes Mountains in South America. He was looking for something special. He believed there was a city of gold in the mountains. He and his group of over 200 men were joined by another Spanish explorer, Francisco de Orellana (oh ray YAHN ah).

Ocean

Amazon River

Madeira River

Francisco de Orellana

The explorers faced many problems and soon ran out of food. Orellana set sail with several men in small boats down the Napo River. The fast-moving river carried them over 700 miles before they found food.

The current was too strong to go back, so they continued down the river. Although they did not know it, the Napo River joined the Amazon River. After 10 months and 3,000 miles, Orellana reached the end of the river where it flows into the Atlantic Ocean. Along the way the Spanish travelers saw parts of the rain forest. It was unlike any land they had ever seen.

■ **The Amazon River is one of the largest and longest rivers in the world.**

During the 1800s the Amazon rain forest became famous for its rubber trees. Natural rubber made from the sap of rubber trees was useful for making many different products.

In more recent times, scientists have visited rain forests to study the animals and plants. One of these early researchers was United States President Theodore "Teddy" Roosevelt. He traveled to Brazil in 1913 to explore the Amazon rain forest with members of the National Geographic Society. They collected examples of living things for the American Museum of Natural History.

■ Teddy Roosevelt

20

Many people from around the world have since visited the rain forests. Scientists are still learning and discovering new things about these lands every day.

Forest Facts

Until the 1900s most people living in the Amazon rain forest had little or no contact with anyone living outside their own area of the forest.

CHAPTER 4

Discovering Rain-Forest Plants

When the first people and later explorers came to the South American rain forest, what did they find? Viewed from above, the rain forest may look like one big forest. But it is actually made up of three layers. These layers are almost like the floors of a building. Each layer has its own special kind of plant and animal life.

■ **View of the rain forest from above**

The "first floor," or bottom layer, is called the *forest floor*. The light here is dim because not much sunlight reaches through the leaves and branches. Bushes, ferns, some vines, and other small plants grow here.

The *understory* is the "second floor," or middle layer. Young trees and palm trees grow in this level. They struggle upward, trying to get as much light as possible.

The "third floor," or top layer, is called the *canopy*. Here grow the big trees from 160 feet to 220 feet tall. The sun shines brightly and it is very hot here.

23

When scientists started coming to the Amazon rain forest, they were amazed by the trees they discovered. One of the largest trees in the rain forest is the kapok (KAY pahk). Reaching above most other trees in the canopy, the kapok can grow up to 180 feet tall. This is about as tall as a 15-story building.

Kapok trees have short, thick trunks and many long branches. When they bloom in the fall, fruits appear that have a white cotton inside. This cotton can be used to stuff mattresses, pillows, furniture, and even life jackets.

Kapok seeds have an oil that is used in making soap and cattle feed. The light, soft wood of kapoks is used to make canoes and rafts. The tree even contains a gum that is used in medicines.

■ Kapok tree

■ Water lilies   ■ Lianas

Some of the tallest plants in the rain forest aren't trees but vines. Called lianas (lee AH nuz), these plants look like ropes dangling from tall trees in the canopy. Lianas sometimes curl around a tree trunk or grow straight down from the branches. Some vines grow longer than 300 feet. That is longer than a football field. Liana vines can be as narrow as a string or as thick as a baseball bat.

The largest water lily pads in the world are found in the rain forest. These plants float in the water and look like large, shallow pans. They can grow to be from two feet to six feet across.

25

The pitcher plant is one of the few plants in the world that eats meat! The plant has tube-shaped or pitcher-shaped leaves that trap insects. If bugs land on a leaf's edge, they slip on the smooth surface. Then they slide down the tube. There they drown in a pool of sticky liquid. After the bugs die, the liquid dissolves them. The insects become food that helps the plant grow.

Rain-forest plants are amazing to see. But perhaps the most important discovery that scientists have made is inside the plants.

■ Pitcher plant

Many rain-forest plants contain substances that can be used to make medicines. These medicines help cure people of many illnesses.

For example, more than 400 years ago, Amerindians in South America used the bark of the cinchona (sihn KOH nuh) tree to lower fevers. Today the bark of the cinchona tree is used to make a drug that treats malaria and other diseases.

■ Cinchona tree

Two drugs that come from the rosy periwinkle plant are used to treat cancer. One of these drugs has been used successfully to fight leukemia (loo KEE mee uh).

People called healers who live in the rain forests know which plants cure sickness. They know from experience which plants to stay away from because they are poisonous. They also know which plants are safe. Their knowledge has helped the rain-forest people for many years. Now scientists are using this knowledge and the plants to help sick people around the world.

Forest Facts

- Only a few thousand of the 250,000 kinds of rain-forest plants have been studied for possible use as medicines.

CHAPTER 5

Discovering Rain-Forest Animals

Besides plants, a wonderful variety of animals has been discovered in the rain forests. For example, on the forest floor in Brazil there are anteaters and tapirs. In the understory live snakes, monkeys, and squirrels. The canopy is home to many birds, large and small.

If you were to walk through the rain forest, you might not see many animals. That's because the animals are hidden or camouflaged. They can see you clearly, but you would have a hard time finding them.

■ Green eyelash viper

29

■ Ocelot

Camouflaged animals have colors and patterns on their skin and fur that help them hide and blend into the rain forest. Frogs might be the same shade of green as the leaf they are sitting on. Bugs often look like sticks. Butterfly wings may look like dried leaves. If the animals don't move, no one can see them.

Camouflage helps many animals hide from other animals that might eat them. It also helps the hunters. A big cat or snake can blend in as it hunts for food. The ocelot has spots that help it to hide in the rain-forest shadows.

When the capybara (kap ee BAH ruh) needs to hide, it wades among water plants. It sinks into the water until only its nose shows.

The capybara is the world's largest rodent. It looks a lot like a guinea pig, but it can weigh up to 100 pounds. That is as heavy as a large dog. In fact, a capybara is often called a water hog. Like all rodents, a capybara has long front teeth. Unlike many rodents, it has webbed toes, which help it to swim well.

Capybaras

In some parts of the rain forest, animals should stay out of the water if piranhas (puh RAHN uz) are swimming there. The piranha is one of the most famous fish in the world. It is also one of the most dangerous.

Piranhas can be small, just 5 to 8 inches long. Others grow to 2 feet. They have razor-sharp teeth. They often feed on other fish. They will attack any animal that is struggling in the water or is injured. When traveling in large schools, or groups, they can kill even a large animal in the water within a few minutes.

Some rain-forest animals have no need for camouflage. For example, tree frogs known as poison-arrow frogs come in many colors. They may be bright red, green, or yellow. The bright colors tell other animals to stay away because the frogs are poisonous.

The poison-arrow frog has a liquid on its skin that is poisonous to other animals. If another animal bites the frog, that animal will become sick and may even die. This frog's poison is so dangerous that rain-forest people have used the liquid to make poison darts.

A poison-arrow frog looks out from a flower.

33

Other colorful rain-forest animals are the birds found there. One half of all the birds in the world live in the rain forest. Some birds spend only the winter there. Others live there all year long. Rain-forest birds can be as small as the hummingbird or as large as the toucan.

Scarlet macaw

The parrots are among the most colorful. Hyacinth macaws and green-winged macaws are a rainbow of bright blue, red, green, and yellow feathers. Parrots usually fly together in flocks, looking for food. They use their hooked bills to pick fruit and to crack seeds.

The toucan's beak is big and looks heavy. However, it is really light in weight. Toucans use their bills to pick and break open ripe fruit.

Keel-billed toucan

Birds share their treetop homes with many kinds of monkeys, squirrels, and bats. One of the most interesting monkeys is the howler monkey. This animal doesn't really howl. But it does make moaning sounds that can be heard from more than a mile away. Sometimes called the opera singer of the rain forest, the howler monkey has a large windpipe in its throat. This windpipe allows it to "sing" loudly.

 **Red howler monkey**

The greatest number of rain-forest creatures are insects. Scientists believe there are between 30 million and 80 million insects in the world's rain forests. These insects include ants, beetles, crickets, cockroaches, and termites.

■ **Amazon leaf-cutter ants**

Forest Facts

- Some rain-forest beetles are no bigger than the period at the end of this sentence.

- Large rain-forest spiders can grow three inches long. Their size makes them big enough to trap small animals.

CHAPTER 6

Meeting Rain-Forest People

When European explorers arrived in the rain forests, they found many human communities. These people had lived in rain forests for thousands of years.

Some rain-forest people today live in villages along the Amazon River, where they farm, hunt, and fish. In their boats they use the river like a highway. Other people live deep within the forest. Their homes, clothing, and ways of getting food are much like the way people lived in the rain forests long ago.

▦ Amazon rain-forest people

In the South American rain forests alone, there are about 200,000 Amerindians. Their ancestors were the first people to live along the Amazon. These people include the Kayapó (kay yuh POH), the Krenak, and the Yanomami (yah nuh MAH mee). Each group has its own way of life and its own language.

Many people in the rain forest live in small villages of about 75 people. Their homes are made with grass and wood. The roofs are made of leaves.

■ **Kayapó village**

■ Yanomami woman preparing bread

For food, the Yanomami gather plants from the forest. Some of the plants they search for are palm fruits, Brazil nuts, and bananas. They also hunt animals, such as small rodents, lizards, and insects. They even grow a few crops.

A favorite time for the Yanomami is when one village invites another village to a feast. People may travel many miles to come to one of these feasts. The guests are given gifts, such as a cooking pot or food. They must then invite their hosts back to their village.

All of the people who live in the world's rain forests are alike in one way. They know the rain forests best.

The biggest problem these people face today is from outsiders who are destroying

Children in a canoe on the Amazon River

their rain-forest homes. Many of the rain-forest people are trying to find ways to protect their forests.

Forest Facts

In 1988, two men from a Kayapó village traveled to Washington, D.C. They asked for help in stopping a dam from being built. The water held by the dam would flood their homes. The men also met with the Brazilian government. To date, the dam has not been built.

CHAPTER 7

The Rain Forest in Danger

The rain forests have existed since the time of the dinosaurs. During the past few hundred years, though, the activities of people from outside the rain forests are threatening to destroy these ancient places. Oil, mining, and logging companies damage huge areas of land. Ranchers cut down forests to make the land into grazing pasture for their cattle. Other people cut down the trees to make roads.

Cattle graze on deforested land.

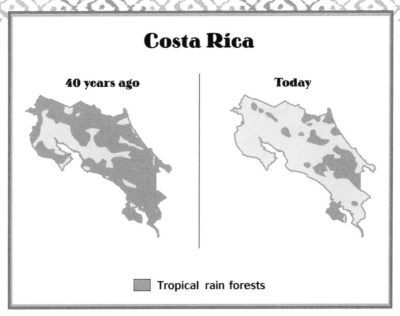

Costa Rica

40 years ago　　　　**Today**

Tropical rain forests

Deforestation of the rain forest in Costa Rica over 40 years

As years go by, more and more rain-forest land is disappearing. For example, almost two thirds of the rain forest in Costa Rica has been destroyed. The same thing will happen to the Amazon rain forest if we are not careful.

As the forests vanish, so do the plants and animals that live in them. Scientists believe that over 100 kinds of living things are wiped out every day. This is thousands of living things each year. If this rate of deforestation continues, almost all of the tropical rain forest will be destroyed by the year 2020.

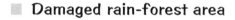

If the rain forests are completely destroyed, the earth will be in terrible trouble. As you have read, healthy rain forests are important to the earth's climate. As the rain forests disappear, the earth will get hotter and more polluted.

In addition, many wonderful plants and animals will disappear forever. The rain-forest people will no longer have a home or food to survive. Many valuable medicines, foods, and other products will also be lost to the world forever.

Damaged rain-forest area

43

Many people around the world are becoming more worried about the vanishing rain forests. Some are trying to do something about it by writing books and songs about the rain forest and by raising money to protect the land.

However, saving the forests is not easy. The land is also important to farmers and ranchers in rain-forest countries who make their living growing crops and raising cattle. Many business people think that cutting down the trees creates jobs for people. Everyone wants to use the rain forests, for many different reasons.

People often ask what they can do to help save the rain forests. The situation is very serious because the rain forests are in great danger. But everyone can help, even in small ways.

◇ **Help protect rain-forest animals and plants that are in danger.** Talk to people about not buying products made of reptile skins, tortoise shells, or cat pelts. It's also important not to buy turtles, birds, or other creatures that are captured and taken from their homes in the rain forests to be sold as pets.

A captured rain-forest parrot

◇ **Buy renewable goods when possible.**
Renewable goods are things made or harvested
from rain-forest plants and other resources
without harming anything. Some of these
products include cereals, cookies, and nuts
harvested from rain-forest trees and plants.
Chocolate, cinnamon, and sugar cane also
come from the rain forests.

■ Heavy traffic on a highway in the United States

◇ **Save energy.**
Oil companies are responsible for some of the destruction of rain-forest land as they look for more oil resources. If people used less gasoline and oil, there would be less need to take oil from the ground where rain forests grow.

◇ **Buy fewer fast-food hamburgers.** The meat is likely to come from cattle raised on land that used to be rain forest. Beef sold in supermarkets is more likely to be from cattle not raised on rain-forest lands.

◇ **Here are more ideas.**
- Recycle whenever possible.
- Buy paper goods made of recycled paper.
- Avoid using throwaway paper products.

As more and more people try to help, some of the rain forests may be saved. From these remaining forests, it might be possible to help destroyed parts grow back. But it takes a long time for a rain forest to grow. So it's important that people act now.

Tree seedling

Just think! Some day you might discover the most amazing rain-forest secret of all.

Forest Facts

Rain-forest soil is very poor. Good soil is made from leaves and dead creatures that decay and leave nutrients. When animals and plants die in the rain forest, their remains are quickly eaten by insects and other things. There is nothing left to make the soil good for farming.

GLOSSARY

atmosphere (AT mus fihr) the layer of gases that surrounds Earth, or all the air around Earth

camouflage (KAM uh flahzh) anything, such as color or shape, that is used as a disguise in nature or to hide something

climate (KLYE mut) the average weather conditions of a place over many years

deforestation (dee for ih STAY shun) the removing of trees or forests from a piece of land

ecosystem (EK oh sihs tum) an area in which living and nonliving things interact

poisonous (POI zuh nus) capable of harming or killing by poison

pollute (puh LOOT) to make unclean

recent (REE sunt) happened lately

recycle (ree SYE kul) to use again and again, or to change to a new use

renewable (rih NOO uh bul) able to be used or made again